Beyond The Next Valley

Beyond The Next Valley

Poems by a Medical Officer in
Papua New Guinea
1972–1974

DAVID HEALEY

The Choir Press

Copyright © 2025 David Healey

All rights reserved. No part of this publication may be reproduced or transmitted in any form or by any means, electronic or mechanical including photocopying, recording or any information storage or retrieval system, without prior permission in writing from the publishers.

The right of David Healey to be identified as the author of this work has been asserted by him in accordance with the Copyright, Designs and Patents Act 1988

First published in the United Kingdom in 2025 by
The Choir Press

ISBN 978-1-78963-555-3

BY THE SAME AUTHOR

Slowing the Afternoon Down

Sleeping Among Yaks

Searching for Cowries

The Radar Girl

Front cover: Chimbu men at Kundiawa sing sing wearing bird-of-paradise head dresses

I dedicate these poems
to my daughter Charlotte and son Theo,
in memory of their mother
Annabel (Anni) Clare Healey;

also to Annabel Loba Rosas,
Theo's daughter and my granddaughter,
and Katie, her mother.

ACKNOWLEDGEMENTS

These poems arose from my daughter, Charlotte Healey, discovering and reading the diaries that my late first wife Annabel and I wrote while in Papua New Guinea between 1972 and 1974. We worked firstly at Kundiawa Hospital in the Chimbu District (now Chimbu province). Later, I became District Medical Officer for Southern Highlands District while she worked for The Leprosy Mission, both of us based in Mendi. I'm extremely grateful to Charlotte and to Theodore, our son, for the interest they have shown in our time spent in the country just prior to its independence under the Crown in 1975.

The poems, written fifty years later, express our feelings while living in the beautiful country, its effect on us and our relationship. They also convey what is lost in the course of time. The country in many areas has changed more markedly than most because of the need for such a newly opened-up nation to catch up with other nations and also because of its recently discovered natural resources. In places where we once visited indigenous people in undisturbed forest there is now deforestation due to timber and oil extraction and the development of new towns and highways.

My role as a medic back in the early seventies was chiefly to fill a gap before a local Papua New Guinean replacement could be found. I'm very grateful to the PNG Department of Public Health and Voluntary Service Overseas for making this possible and also for the support of Doctors Kevin Farrell and Penelope Key, Richard Longley and the then matron of Kundiawa Hospital, Robin. Also a big thank you to all the kiaps, health extension officers and missionaries I met during our visits to various outstations, especially Keith and his wife at the Bosavi Mission. I should also like to thank Ongogo, our Chimbu *haus boi*, and his family.

I obtained a lot of information on the history of early patrols from James Sinclair's books, especially *The Outside Man: Jack Hides of Papua.*

Lastly, I would like to thank Nicola Healey, The East Suffolk Poetry Group and Anna Davidson for their help and advice. Any mistakes found are mine and mine only. I'd like to thank Ann, my wife, for all her support and toleration of the time I've spent writing these poems.

A NOTE ON MELANESIAN PIDGIN

The pidgin language I include in some of the poems is as close as possible to that spoken and written at the time we were in the Chimbu District (now a province more frequently spelled Simbu) and in the Southern Highlands. It also tries to match the pidgin of the 1971 first edition of The Jacaranda Dictionary and Grammar of Melanesian Pidgin by F. Mihalic. I suspect there is some personal and regional variation which I'm unable to decipher or to own up to. Time has also caused changes and an expansion to what originally was a despised trade jargon and is now a respected and indispensable lingua franca to over a million people.

CONTENTS

Acknowlegements	vii
Prologue	xiii
The Unknown	1
Flying Over The Waghi	2
Your First Days In Kundiawa	4
Triage	5
Haemorrhage	6
Osteomyelitis	8
Pig- Bel	9
The Malnutrition Hut	10
Betel Nut	11
Expats	12
Villages	13
The Motor Bike	14
Vegemite	15
Bush Tucker	16
Bosavi	18
Bathing At Bosavi	19
Family Planning	20

Where The Trees End	22
Contact	24
Culture Shock	26
The Lake	28

PROLOGUE

Many modern-day Papua New Guineans have good reason to feel somewhat resentful towards outsiders who opened up their country, particularly when self- interest played a part in the search for gold and other mineral resources such as copper and oil. However, Australia, who governed the whole country from the end of the First World War until independence in 1975, could be seen as a relatively benign-colonising nation compared to many others in the past. The Australian administration was relatively sensitive to the needs of indigenous people, which historically was not always the case in their treatment of First Nations People in their own country.

The 'Outside Men' are the Australian explorers of the 1920s and 30s, such as Ivan Champion, Bill Adamson, Jim O'Malley, Jack Hides and the Leahy brothers, to name but a few, who didn't always receive good publicity from other patrol officers, governors or the press. The first poem, 'The Unknown' is based on James Sinclair's account of the early months of the Hides and O'Malley 1934–35 expedition into the unknown Western Division. It was the last patrol in New Guinea not to have the benefit of a prior aerial inspection of the terrain or of radio communication. It's easy now in retrospect to be critical of some of their aims and attitudes and to judge them harshly in the light of today's values. However, the early explorers were usually careful not to harm tribesmen encountered when venturing into unknown parts of the territory. Deaths usually resulted from misunderstanding and self-defence.

Tribute should also be paid to the work and endurance of indigenous policemen, carriers and medical orderlies during these early patrols. Years later, during our own stay in Papua New Guinea, we witnessed first-hand the work of indigenous health extension officers in remote areas. They saved many more lives – by treating pneumonia with long-acting injectable penicillin and malaria by judicious use of anti-malarials, and by fulfilling vaccination programmes – than European and Australian doctors working in the district hospitals.

The Unknown

After leaving supplies up the Strickland
the patrol paddled slowly up the Rentoul
until stopped by rapids. They then burnt
most of their canoes to discourage deserters.

For weeks they cut through virgin forest
with bush knives, so carriers could follow,
coming across friendly or hostile tribesmen
and running low on rice and tinned meat.

Hungry and exhausted in the early months
they often wanted to turn back, even when
it was too late to do so, not knowing what
lay ahead, what food they would find to eat.

The tribesmen they met refused gifts of cloth,
bush knives and tomahawks and wanted
instead mother-of-pearl and cowries
that the patrol hadn't brought with them.

The Great Limestone Barrier blocked
their way: fissures, craters and sink holes.
Sometimes they only managed to advance
three miles a day. There were injuries.

Eventually, they reached a valley of rising
smoke trails; the people provided pig meat
and sweet potato; for a while there was no
dodging spears or firing Lee-Enfield rifles.

Flying Over The Wahgi

Gold mining was Dan Leahy's
priority and later coffee
when alluvial gold ran out.
The eighth of nine children
he disappointed his Irish-born
parents who wanted more
for him than an uncertain
future in the mandated territory
of Papua New Guinea.

On March 8, 1933,
with two of his brothers
he flew over the highlands
to the centre of the island
discovering a great flat valley
teeming with nests
of oblong grass houses
and gardens resembling
patchwork fields in Belgium.

The gasoline fuel indicator
forced them to return.
They were front-page-news
within days in a world
that had never suspected
so many new people existed
in such a remote region,
seemingly organised
far from modern man.

It was forty years before
we flew over the same view.
I held a paper bag full of vomit
and you were tightening
your belt in the turbulence,
more scared by the flight
than you ever were encountering
rows of armed and painted
Chimbus stamping their feet.

Your First Days In Kundiawa

Our bungalow was next to The Paradise Club where trucks
stopped and started and dogs barked most of the night.

We vowed not to have servants but it wasn't long before
we had a Chimbu cleaner, cook and self-appointed gardener.

Aussie wives invited you to help them with charity tombolas;
it was kind, but wasn't what you'd come all this way to do.

It took a puncture on patrol with a community nurse
to make you feel you'd arrived in New Guinea at last.

You were invisible to aircraft as the canopy was dense.
A bridge was down due to flooding after you crossed.

You had no radio. Children gathered round you while men
with spears stood close-by and the women welcomed you.

Triage

They arrived from Kerowagi
by truck, spears still in situ.
Abdomen and chest injuries
came first, were stretchered off,
triaged and cross-matched.
The walking-injured stepped
down to wait on the grass
where wounds were cleansed.
Barbs held fast; they needed
removing in the minor ops
shed, but had to wait.
Those with buttock wounds
wanted large keloid scars
to show off their valour
even though they'd run away.

There was no let-up in the days
that followed. Post-operative
complications interrupted our
getting through the patients.
The numbers were building up.
One or two, with deep wounds
that were difficult to clean,
developed tetanus spasms;
we paralysed their muscles
and took over their breathing.
We did things by reading how,
radioing Goroka for advice
while running low on staff,
drugs and anaesthetics,
expertise, energy and sleep.

Haemorrhage

We couldn't afford to waste time.
A *Hammett's Abdominal Surgery*
was held open at the right place.
The operation appeared simple:

quick incision, double ligature,
drain in situ to be on the safe side
then out. Job done but it wasn't:
blood welled up, blood pressure

dropped. The mask was put back
on his face and IV fluid increased.
Sweat dripped from my forehead
and my spectacles steamed up.

Onga, the *dokta boi*, took over,
his hands peeling back bowel
to where he found the cause
and tied knots to stop the leak.

Onga saved the day, saved my skin.
Outside, the patient's wife
and their children were waiting.
Would *katim rausim pen olgeta?*

Pigs squealed from poinsettia
bushes on the hill. Pitohuis
called from the Casuarina trees
as if nothing had happened.

More sick were arriving. A low
musical murmuring began.
Spirit-song. Stories being told.
An earth tremor spilt my coffee.

---

dokta boi local medical assistant
katim rausim pen olgeta? operation get rid of pain altogether?

Osteomyelitis

This time I had to operate: clear away infected bone
and loose debris; then give a long course of antibiotics.
In the weeks that followed

Kema sat with his mother down by the river in the shade
of a Casuarina tree. They liked to feed the birds
which Chimbus don't usually do;

instead they shoot them with three-pronged arrows
then cook them in hot ash. Kema also learnt to write
English on pieces of bark.

When I visited, their smiles brought me some relief
from the steady stream of patients, the long hours spent
in theatre and not being sure

I was up to the job. Cicadas kept me awake at night
and an old petrol generator didn't help either.
Radio reception for advice

was poor but there was no breakdown of signals between
Kema, his mother and me. They taught me the names
of birds in their language

that sounded the same as their calls: no need for Greek
nomenclature or burdening birds-of-paradise with titles
of count, archduke or princess.

When Kema and his mother left they gave me an amulet
of pig hide carved with zigzag patterns. His healed leg
made my mind up to stay.

Pig-Bel

I didn't think Epi's talks in the villages
would make a difference but fewer cases
were reported since her project began,

since she showed them pictures of men,
women and children in pain after eating
under-cooked pork days after a pig-kill.

She pointed out how to prevent pig-bel:
covering food to stop flies landing on it,
hand-washing and eating more protein.

I dreaded what I'd find inside one boy,
opening him up when an X-ray showed
air under the diaphragm, a diagnosis

of perforation due to necrotising enteritis.
Happily, just a few lengths of gut needed
resecting, the rest looked healthy enough.

After a stormy post-op of drainage, drip
and suck, she thanked me for helping
her *wantok*. We didn't argue anymore.

She hoped we'd work closer together
in the future. Neither of us dared admit
what we really felt about each other.

---

wantok belonging to the same talk or tribe

The Malnutrition Hut

It was my temporary refuge back then,
believe it or not, a place of calm activity,
feeding and fluid replacement to keep
babies alive, an escape from the main
haus sik, its long queues. And despite
being white, having no scars, tattoos
and ornaments and wearing clean shorts,
the mothers got used to me, and became
less wary when I examined their child.

The local nurses were better than me
at setting up drips, quicker too: scalp vein
needles, fixed in place by plaster of Paris,
delivered half-strength Darrow's solution.
Most of the babies had stick-like arms,
swollen bellies, sores and oral thrush.
Each day I checked for breathlessness,
listened for crepitations in their chests.
Breathing couldn't be taken for granted.

We celebrated weight gain, a first smile,
but dreaded the day they went home.
News from their villages wasn't good.
There were fights, famine and cargo cults.
Maternal large spleens meant malaria
was rife. Hookworm counts were high.
There was no certainty of follow-up care,
their survival or being free of side effects.
What benefits did I bring? What harm?

---

haus sik hospital

Betel Nut

A trail of red splashes lay
on the road to the *haus sik*.
I thought they might be blood
when I first saw them;
only later, looking into the mouth
of a man clearly off his trolley,
did I see a red paste.

He was found collapsed
according to records and hearsay.
A *dokta boi* recognised him
as Onga, a nut addict,
previously *bikpela man planti pigs*
now living by a crooked path
that leads nowhere –

good walking country for us
high above the valley
and that's when I met him again.
He showed us his two sons,
a daughter with her new baby
and his mother who we treated
for pneumonia last month.

Then he took us to a ridge
where Raggiana birds-of-paradise
were displaying in tree tops,
three males appealing to a hen bird.
Their red tail coverts, spread out,
were raised and lowered
then raised again.

---

bikpela man planti pigs important man with plenty of pigs

Expats

The term applied not to those from down south
but to Europeans like Hans, a doctor from Hamburg,
who worked for six months filling gaps and thought
Chimbus short-changed by the Aussie administration.

There were missionaries from Holland and Germany,
a Czech refugee engineer, a lady from Connemara
who ran a woman's refuge, and drifters like Ned
who didn't want it known where they came from.

Then, there were those from the UK either in love
with Papuans, depressed or going bush, who crashed
out at our place at weekends, drank our Foster's lager
and talked of abiding love, break-ups and loneliness.

You acted as counsellor as none were around, fielded
their anger towards mum, dad, brother or sister
or the difficulty they had with men, women or both.
Some craved a good discussion whatever the subject.

We had unsorted hang-ups of our own: believing
we could change the world when we knew nothing
about it, never thinking we'd go wrong, never
wondering why it was we had so many nightmares.

We thought our good intentions were enough,
that not flaunting what we own, not exacting a price,
would go down well with Chimbus. I only had one
wife. We made no children. They weren't impressed.

Villages

They may just as well have been Alf, May, Beth and Dud
at Boyton, back in Cornwall, where I used to stop my bike
for a chat and cup of tea:

Asa, Wen, Ata and Gona enjoying small talk with me
asking *hamas pikinini bilong yupela?* and *hamas taim
i stap long Nuigini?*

They were openly friendly for no other reason
than they wanted to be. It was twenty years since Jules,
the Lutheran missionary,

had entered their village to bring them the Good News.
Tribal fighting continued but deaths were limited
by pay-back agreements.

Most had never been outside their valley. For them
the rest of the world was peopled with ghosts, ancestors
and magic men with *planti kago*.

Not so Gona's son who studied law at Moresby Uni
and often returned home for *singsings* and pig-kills.
He knew its dangers: guns, drugs,

the false promises of cargo-cults, mining companies
and artefact traders. He'd seen the newsreels of B-52s
blanket bombing villages in Vietnam.

---

hamas pikinini bilong yupela? how many children do you have?
hamas taim i stap long Nuigini? how long are you staying in New Guinea?
planti kago plenty of cargo

The Motor Bike

Its oval silver petrol tank they thought was an egg.
Its double exhaust an exit for venomous spirits.

Last night, the Kawasaki one thousand ccs shot
moonlight at darkness with the kiap on its back

driving round and round the compound singing
My Sweet Lord though it was George Harrison's

voice we heard through all the crackles and jumps
of his scratched single and hum of the speakers.

Next day, several villagers from beyond the gorge
were nowhere to be seen. Some said they'd retreated

into further bush; others, that they had followed
the river to the coast for bikes of their own.

Weeks later they were found, thin and exhausted
beside an airstrip they had built for a plane to land

bringing all the cargo promised by a spirit man
from Koroba, including bikes and sound systems.

---

kiap resident administration officer

Vegemite

It tasted awful the first week
but by the second we were hooked,
spreading it thinly on toast
then more thickly.

We added a teaspoon to stir fries,
to leftover sweet potato and beans
and took it on patrol with us
as a vital ingredient.

You'll not get beriberi with Vegemite,
the kiap Shane told us,
but going back to Marmite
will kill you.

Made in Melbourne since 1922
Vegemite takes me back to the Wahgi,
to *The Dark Side of The Moon,*
our only LP

played over and over again
before Sky television and streaming,
before social media replaced
writing letters home.

Bush Tucker

Hot stones
beneath soil.
Leaves wrapped round kebabs
of some sort:

roasted cassowary?
barramundi, fresh or salt water?
or pig pieces?
Smelt good.

The missionary
said grace
thanking the Lord
for what He provides

then encouraged me
to eat whatever it was.
Went well
with my reconstituted

Smash
and Knorr's vegetable soup.
Tasted like tofu
soaked in chicken Oxo.

Next day Kata
scraped swollen
Michelin-tyre-looking bugs
from bark

stripped from its tree –
planti gutpela kai kai,
this time, raw,
this time, wriggling.

---

planti gutpela kai kai plenty good food

Bosavi

It was your hair they wanted to feel,
long and silky after you washed it
with Silvikrin in a clear stream
that morning several valleys away.

A woman wearing many beads
approached you first, blew through
her pursed lips and turned to others
as if singing to them a story.

Others came slowly forward to touch
your breasts. The missionary told us
they'd never seen a white woman
before; his own wife had never been

this far away from the Mission.
They asked why it was you were thin
expecting you to be much fatter,
have children and look like the Queen.

Bathing At Bosavi

If only I had told you then and there
in the clear stream that was deep enough
for our bodies to immerse in completely
and cool ourselves down. We wiped away
dark smudges of squashed mosquitoes
from exposed skin, keeping our shorts
and T-shirts on should anyone be watching.
I could have said *how much I loved you*

but instead I imitated Stewart Granger
and saw you as Deborah Kerr in the film
King Solomon's Mines while imagining
its jumpy soundtrack and underwater
-sounding background orchestral music.
I splashed you, watching your breasts
leap in unison with your fake protest.
If only I had held you then and told you.

Iridescent turquoise butterflies landed
on your T-shirt, the same colour as them,
and green ones on your emerald shorts.
We could have remained there as they
opened and closed their wings on us
but I waded to the bank instead, away
from the sun shining on us in mid-stream,
thinking there'd always be another chance.

Family Planning

The pilot of our single-prop
wasn't the most reassuring Aussie.
You poms don't know the half of it.
If the bush don't kill you
the death adders will.

I had fifteen intrauterine coils
to fit at the Protestant Mission.
Each women wanted to stop
having a baby every year,
to give her body a rest

already anaemic from childbirth
blood loss, hookworm and malaria.
Half their children die
of gastroenteritis and pneumonia
before age five.

Three months later the same pilot
took me to their follow-up,
this time calling me *Dave* not *doc*.
His *sheila* and him had
recently split up.

The news wasn't good. Most devices
had vanished from their wombs.
Perhaps I'd left the strings too long
and the coils could easily
be pulled out.

Their husbands might have done it,
or a village *tambaranman*
opposed to white man's magic
or the Catholic Mission
at the other end of the airstrip.

---

tambaranman a man in league with the spirits

Where The Trees End

The helicopter used for the famine drop at Kandep
picked up Neto, his mum and me on its flight back
to Moresby. A tumour in his neck was making it
difficult for him to breathe.

We skirted Mount Karimui where ribbons of water
fell from the broken-bottle rim of the crater.
After an hour flying over the forest we looked
down on houses and grass.

He'd never seen cars and lorries before. They moved
along snake-like paths he was told were roads.
He stayed where he was after we landed, frightened
to step on the ladder.

Everything was noisy and travelling fast. A giant plane
with no propellers roared off the ground. Fireflies
filled the inside of the ambulance. At the hospital
we tried to stay with him.

In X-ray, Neto saw what looked like the shadow
of his grandpa's skull kept displayed on a platform
back in their village, and next day he told us
a mask put him to sleep.

Months later, a bow and arrow was back in his hands
but at night Neto woke screaming and pleaded
for things to slow down. He dreamed he was falling
off the edge of the world.

His mother couldn't get him to eat. The ancestors
weren't happy according to those in the *tambaran haus*.
Evil spirits had entered his body and were trapped
by his long thick scar.

---

tambaran haus village spirit house

Contact

We came across them on the tenth
day of our patrol. They were wearing
arse-grass, wigs of cassowary feathers
and curved gourds on their penises.
Many, I could see, had skin infections,
large spleens from chronic malaria
and distended abdomens due to worms.
Even if they did let me take their blood
we were too far from any laboratory.
Besides, they had spears and stone axes;
it wouldn't take long for one of them
to up-the-ante and *mi bagarup pinis*.

One of them peered inside the bell
of my stethoscope, then placed it
on his chest: *crackles* he said after me
when I told him what I heard inside.
Women emerged from trees behind.
Some were pregnant; others emaciated.
There was no going back the kiap told me
with oilmen, missionaries and traders
in the area. TB and whooping cough
were reported. We needed to immunise
as soon as possible, convince them
lik lik spia givim gutpela marasin.

On day twelve, we heard chainsaws
in the forest. There was too much smoke.
A body was seen floating down river.
Sulphur-crested cockatoos flew over us
and a flock of parakeets broke cover.
Some person held out a withered arm,
another showed me his crooked leg
and one touched me so lightly I nearly
didn't feel it. A child with oedema
and broken-enamel skin stepped
back from me should I cause him
further distress. Deficiencies thrived.

---

mi bagarup pinis I get killed

lik lik spia givim gutpela marasin needle give good medicine

Culture Shock

There was a lot to get used to: the heat,
sharp rubble on the roads that bruised
our toes because we wore flip-flops,
Chimbus chatting under our bungalow
when it rained and the truck revving up
as it climbed to collect me on a night call.

You had giardiasis our first two months
while I was out of my depth coping
after Kevin Farrell left for the Sepik.
Cases kept coming. We argued a lot.
Then your health improved and I learnt
from *dokta bois* simpler, safer procedures.

You carried *kaukau*, papaya and maize
in a *bilum* on your back but without the baby
and firewood Chimbu mothers also carried.
You joked with them about men, made
friends with a subversive Aussie matron
and set up a guest house for VSOs.

Two years later, our return to England
was more distressing with rush hours,
careers, mortgages and the expectation
we'd start a family. There was no escaping
protocols, form-filling and referrals
to outpatients with long waiting lists.

The planet beneath our feet felt fixed.
So much was organised invisibly
at a distance without smiles, greetings
or stories. We even missed earth tremors
spilling our tea and the mozzie bites
we eased by sitting under waterfalls.

---

dokta bois local medical assistants
kaukau sweet potato
bilum string bag made of foraged natural fibres

The Lake

i.m. Anni Healey

You rapidly departed that night
though your body kept on living
for a few more hours. I felt
a sudden rush of air take you
out through the bedroom window,
wide open in a heat wave.
You went back to New Guinea
as a twenty-something, wearing
the same shorts and batik top
in the photograph of us
on your crowded locker –

we're sitting in a dugout
with tribesmen on a village-
to-village TB patrol of the lake
tape recording their *tok tok*.
They sing a song about you
stepping on and waking up
a snake, and they imitate me
startled by a large leaping fish.
One of them wears a Man U
shirt, another an armband
made from a Pacific salmon tin.

We lived in London so must
have had tea with the Queen.
There aren't any crocodiles
we're told, though there's no way
of knowing for sure. Nor must
we worry about the Sengi tribe
who it's said no longer eat people.
The dead have different voices
like the birds-of-paradise.
You step ashore and walk
too far ahead; I can't keep up.

---

tok tok conversation

www.ingramcontent.com/pod-product-compliance
Lightning Source LLC
LaVergne TN
LVHW041502070426
835507LV00009B/754